CHAMPIONS
OF
MATHEMATICS

BY
JOHN HUDSON TINER

Master
Books

First printing: March 2000

Copyright © 1999 by Master Books, Inc. All rights reserved.
No part of this book may be used or reproduced in any
manner whatsoever without written permission of the pub-
lisher, except in the case of brief quotations in articles and
reviews. For information write: Master Books, Inc., P.O. Box
727, Green Forest, AR 72638.

ISBN: 0-89051-279-5
Library of Congress Number: 00-100253

Cover by Farewell Communications

Printed in the United States of America

Please visit our website for other great titles:
www.masterbooks.net

For information regarding publicity for author interviews,
contact Dianna Fletcher at (870) 438-5288.

This book is dedicated
to
William C. Heady

CONTENTS

1. The Mathematics of Music 7

2. The Building Blocks of Geometry 15

3. The Sand Reckoner 23

4. Mathematics in Eclipse 27

5. On the Shoulders of Giants 33

6. A Family of Mathematicians 43

7. A Father and Son Tragedy 47

8. The Blind Master 55

9. Prince of Mathematicians 63

Index 71

1

THE MATHEMATICS
OF MUSIC

Pythagoras was one of the first great mathematicians whose name is known. He lived about 2,500 years ago, and he was born on the island of Sámos in the Aegean Sea. Sámos is the nearest island to Turkey on the mainland. During Pythagoras' day, it was one of the leading Greek cities and a successful shipping center. It had a good trade with Egypt and Libya in Northern Africa and with Corinth and other cities in Asia Minor.

Pythagoras' father was a merchant, originally from Tyre (a Phoencian city now part of Lebanon). Tyre was frequently mentioned in the Bible. Hiram, king of Tyre, furnished building materials for Solomon's Temple (1 Kings 9:11). This was about 500 years before the time of Pythagoras. Jesus visited the area around Tyre (Mark 7:24). This was about 500 years after Pythagoras lived.

Pythagoras traveled with his father who bought and sold grain. Their journeys took them as far north as Italy and as far south as Syria. Few other people visited so many interesting places.

He enjoyed playing the lyre and reading poetry. He memorized parts of the great heroic tales by Homer about events surrounding the Trojan wars. Pythagoras, like so many before and after, was thrilled by the exploits of Achilles, the greatest of the Greek warriors. He read about the Greek gift of the wooden Trojan horse, filled with soldiers, that gained entry inside the walled city of Troy. He followed the trials of brave Odesseus in his wandering and when he regained his home after the war.

Pythagoras had an interest in learning. He coined the word "philosophy," which means love of knowledge. Until recently, scientists were known as natural philosophers. A natural philosopher was a person who attempted to understand the natural world. Not only was Pythagoras one of the first scientists, but he coined the name by which they were known.

He visited Miletus, a rival city to Samos, and there met the legendary Thales, the first of the Greek scientists. In astronomy, Thales predicted an eclipse of the sun a year before the event. The eclipse took place on May 28, 585 B.C. The date is known so well because the frightful spectacle halted two armies (the Medes and Lydians) as they advanced to war.

Thales also showed a simple way to measure the height of tall buildings. He took a stick of known length and measured the length of its shadow. Then he compared its length to the length of the shadow of the building. The ratio of the one to the other gave the missing height. Thales measured the height of the pyramids in this way. He measured the length of the shadow of the Great Pyramid of Giza, and it was 214 cubits long. A measuring rod that is six cubits high casts a shadow of four cubits. A simple calculation of the proportion (pyramid height / length of pyramid shadow = rod height / length of rod shadow = pyramid height / 214 = 6/4) gave the height of the pyramid as 321 cubits. Multiply 214 by 6 and divide by 4. A cubit is 18 inches, so the pyramid was a little more than 481 feet high.

This idea of ratios and proportion impressed Pythagoras. He began applying numbers to other areas of science. Thales advised him to study in Egypt. Pythagoras traveled to Egypt. He was taken prisoner when Persia invaded that country. He was carried off to Babylon (now modern day Baghdad in Iraq). Pythagoras took the opportunity to learn more about astronomy from his captors. After five years he gained his freedom and returned home.

About 530 B.C., he settled in Crotona (now Crotone), a Greek colony in southern Italy. He founded a school and tested his ideas about how people should conduct their lives. He wore simple clothes and avoided a show of wealth. He encouraged students to examine themselves and identify their thoughts and emotions.

Pythagoras may have written books, but none of them survive today. His students took notes of his lectures and added to them. It is sometimes difficult to separate his ideas from those of his students.

Scientists do know that he emphasized the role of numbers in describing the natural world. He studied music and sound. His discoveries are surprisingly accurate and still true today.

In almost all of the other sciences — astronomy, physics, biology, chemistry, and medicine — the ideas expressed by the ancient Greeks have proven to be incomplete or in error.

The exception is mathematics. The ideas of Pythagoras and the other Greek mathematics such as Euclid have endured to this present time. Pythagoras was not only correct in mathematics, but also his study of numbers as the foundation of musical tones has proven to be correct, too.

Pythagoras noted that musical tones were more pleasing when the strings vibrated in sections that were ratios of whole numbers. A string of a lyre produced sound because of the vibration of the string. Suppose the entire string vibrated. Then it produced a low tone known as the fundamental pitch. If it were touched in the middle, the string would vibrate in two parts. The pitch would be twice as great as the fundamental. It was the first overtone. If the string were touched near the top, it would vibrate in three parts and produce the second overtone. If two strings vibrated in simple multiples of one another such as 2 to 3, this also gave a pleasing tone. His study of the mathematics of music is one branch of science that has remained

unchanged into modern times.

Pythagoras was a good musician, and would play for students who were ill, to improve their spirits. People of that time often turned to music to soothe their troubled minds. The Bible tells that David in the Old Testament was a musician who played for King Saul. "David would take his harp and play. Then relief would come to Saul; he would feel better" (1 Sam. 16:23).

Pythagoras was fascinated by numbers and identified their special properties. To him, each number had a personality of its own. He arranged pebbles to represent numbers as triangles, squares, or other shapes.

The number three he visualized as a triangle of pebbles. Three can be shown as a single pebble on top and then a row of two pebbles. Ten was a triangle of pebbles. One pebble on top, two in the second row, three in

These 15th century Italian woodcuts imagine Pythagoras proving his ideas of harmony by various tests on bells and on glasses of water (top), on string tensions (middle), and on lengths of columns of air (bottom).

the third row and four in the final row: $1 + 2 + 3 + 4 = 10$.

Four was a square number. It could be written as two rows of two pebbles in the shape of a square. Nine was the next square, three rows of three pebbles.

Some numbers were prime, such as seven, and could not be divided by any other number except one. Others were composite, such as 12, which had many divisors. He called 28 a perfect number because it was the sum of its divisors: $1 + 2 + 4 + 7 + 14 = 28$.

His best-known achievement was the proof of what is today called the Pythagorean theorem. A theorem is a statement that can be proven mathematically correct. The Pythagorean theorem states that the sum of the squares of the legs of a right triangle is equal to the square of the hypotenuse.

Many ancient people had learned this simple rule relating the three sides of a right triangle. A right triangle is one that has one angle of 90 degrees. The two lines connected to the right angle are the legs. The side opposite the 90-degree angle is the hypotenuse. Ancient engineers knew that the sum of the squares of the length of the legs equaled the square of the hypotenuse.

For instance, suppose a right triangle has legs of lengths three and four. The hypotenuse will have a length of five because $3^2 + 4^2 = 5^2$. The superscript 2 means to multiply the number by itself: $3 * 3 + 4 * 4 = 9 + 16 = 25$.

The Egyptians made a practical application of the Pythagorean theorem by taking a cord and knotting it at 12 equally spaced intervals. They held the cord in the shape of a triangle so that one side had three knots and the other side four knots. The last side would have five knots and the angle opposite that side would be a right angle. It helped them lay out their buildings with square corners. The use of the knotted cord was a successful rule of thumb discovered by trial and error.

Pythagoras saw a difference between trial and error and true scientific proof. Pythagoras gave a proof of the Pythagorean theorem. When Pythagoras lived, the notation for showing numbers that we use today had not been invented. Instead, letters of the alphabet stood for numbers. The Greek letter delta, D, represented 10, the Greek letter H represented 100, and the Greek letter chi V represented 1,000. This was a clumsy system and one that was difficult to use.

Rather than proving the Pythagorean theorem with numbers, Pythagoras used geometric figures. He constructed two squares with sides the same lengths as the two sides of the triangle. He showed that their combined area (enclosed space) would equal the area of a square with sides the length of the hypotenuse.

Pythagoras believed that everything could be represented as the ratio of whole numbers. For instance, the pleasing tones of musical instruments were ratios of 1 to 2, 1 to 3, or some other ratio of simple whole numbers. The ratio of the legs of the right triangle that the Egyptians used was 3 to 4.

He believed the common whole numbers (1, 2, 3, 4, and so on) and the fractions formed by them (1/2, 1/3, 2/3, 1/4, 3/4, and so on) could measure all quantities in mathematics and nature. Numbers formed by the ratio of whole numbers are called rational numbers. Pythagoras believed all numbers were rational.

He proved himself wrong while studying the diagonal of a square. The sides of a square are the same lengths. The diagonal of a square is a straight line that connects one corner of the square to the opposite corner and goes through the center of the square. What is the length of the diagonal compared to the sides of the square?

The Pythagorean theorem gives the answer. The diagonal separates the square into two identical right triangles. The legs of the triangle are sides of the square and the hypotenuse of the triangle is the diagonal of the square.

The Pythagorean triangle gives the length of the diagonal by the equation $side^2 + side^2 = diagonal^2$. Suppose the sides of the square have a length of one. When one is squared (multiplied by itself) the answer is one: $1^2 = 1 * 1 = 1$. The length of the diagonal, represented by x, is given by $1^2 + 1^2 = x^2$, or $1 + 1 = x^2$, or $2 = x^2$.

Pythagoras tried to determine what ratio for x, when multiplied by itself, would give 2. The number 10/7 is close because $(10/7)^2 = 100/49$ or about 2.04. That is close but not exact. In fact, no ratio, when multiplied by itself will give two exactly. Rather than being a rational number, the square root of 2 is an irrational number. Irrational means without a ratio. No ratio or decimal fraction can equal it exactly.

This unexpected discovery of irrational numbers was so astonishing that Pythagoras and his students kept it secret for many years. Eventually, the proof was made public and other irrational numbers were discovered. For instance, the ratio of the distance around a circle (circumference) divided by the distance through the center of the circle (diameter) is irrational. It is represented by the Greek letter pi, π. It can be approximated by the ratio 22/7 (about 3.14), but like the square root of 2, pi cannot be given exactly by the ratio of two whole numbers.

In astronomy, Pythagoras stated that the earth was spherical and not flat. He realized that the morning and evening star were the same body (Venus.) He thought numbers controlled the crystalline spheres that gave planets their motions. He tried to relate this motion to the simple ratios of music. The planets do follow simple numeric laws, but not those from music. Pythagoras' idea of music of the spheres put astronomers on the wrong track for many years.

Pythagoras had selected the Greek city of Crotona for his school to avoid political turmoil and to be safe from advancing armies and wars. However, he and his students with their secrecy, unusual dress, and different ways were not entirely accepted by the local inhabitants. They were viewed as a cult and came under persecution. The last days of Pythagoras are unclear. Many scholars believe he fled to Megapontum, a Greek city in southern Italy, where he died.

Exactly how he died is not clear. What is clear is that he made two important advances in mathematics. First, Pythagoras set the standard that mathematical results must be based on mathematical proof, not rules of thumb or vague ideas of what seems reasonable.

Second, when he thought his understanding of mathematics was complete, he discovered irrational numbers. The Bible, in Job chapters 38 and 39, contains a list of questions to show the richness of God's creation and the challenge of learning about the physical world. Time and again, mathematicians and scientists would think they had completely revealed a subject only to be proven wrong by a new discovery. Pythagoras was one of the first to learn this important lesson.

Pythagoras also noticed the harmony in nature. Everything fit together with a unity in the design. Great achievers in science and mathematics have noticed this fact over and over. Great mathematicians who came later such as Isaac Newton and Carl Gauss would recognize the design as being put there by the Creator. Pythagoras was a pagan who did not have access to the Word of God. But even in his ignorance, he saw the hand of the Creator in his studies.

2

THE BUILDING BLOCKS OF GEOMETRY

Science textbooks change yearly as scientists bring new information to light. In other fields, such as history or language, textbooks must be kept up to date, too. A textbook more than 100 years old is hopelessly out-of-date. Yet, one science textbook has stood the test of time for more than 2,000 years — Euclid's *Elements of Geometry*.

In various translations, the book has been in use for centuries. Great scientists such as Isaac Newton and Albert Einstein learned geometry from Euclid's book, as did military leaders such as Julius Caesar and George Washington. *Elements of Geometry* is the most successful textbook of all time. Students everywhere are encouraged to study Euclid because it strengthens their ability to think and reason. Some scholars believe Euclid's *Elements* is the second most translated, published, and studied book of all time. The Bible is first, of course.

Although his book is well known, details of Euclid's life are shrouded in mystery. He was born about 325 B.C. Even the place of his birth cannot be placed exactly. At the time, Euclid was a common name. Historians often confused Euclid with other people who had the same name. For years, historians believed Euclid was born in Megara, along the coast west of Athens. However, later research showed Euclid

Euclid

of Megara was not the one who wrote *Elements*.
From the style of his writing, Euclid probably attended Plato's academy in Athens. Plato lived before Euclid's time, but scholars trained by Plato continued his school. The academy provided a thorough education in a variety of subjects including astronomy, mathematics, political science, and philosophy. Like Plato, the teachers at the academy probably did not regard science as highly as they did the other subjects. They did approve of mathematics and geometry. Euclid received a good grounding in those subjects.

After his study in Athens, Euclid moved to Alexandria. Although in Egypt, Alexandria was a Greek City. The Greek general Ptolemy ruled Alexandria and parts of Egypt and Libya.

Ptolemy had big plans for Alexandria. His goal was to make this city the center of Greek scholarship and science. He built a combination of university, museum, and library in Alexandria. Ships that docked in the harbor and caravans that passed through the city were searched for books and maps. Ptolemy ordered that interesting documents be copied before being returned to their owners. Soon, Alexandria had the greatest library in the world. Until then, Athens was the chief Greek city. The other generals quarreled among themselves. Their battles took place in Greece and weakened Athens.

Ptolemy realized that great people, not books or buildings alone, would make Alexandria a center of Greek learning. He invited scientists to come to Alexandria and live under his protection. Scientists fled from the fighting in Greece and came to Egypt. Almost from the start, Alexandria eclipsed Athens.

Euclid was one of the scientists who moved to Alexandria where he lived under the protection of Ptolemy. In that city, he taught mathematics and geometry.

Once, a student could see no benefit in learning about geometry. The student asked, "What do I get by learning these things?"

Euclid called a slave and said, "Give him a coin, since he must make a gain out of what he learns."

Euclid studied prime numbers. A prime number can be divided exactly by itself and 1, but division by any other number gives a remainder. The first few prime numbers are 2, 3, 5, 7, 11 and 13. Is 15 prime? No, because 3 and 5 will divide it. Is 17 prime? Yes, because it can be divided exactly only by 1 and 17.

At first, prime numbers are relatively common. However, as you go higher and higher, they become more scarce. A total of 25 numbers between 1 and 100 are prime. Between 1,001 and 1,100 only 16 numbers are prime. In general, prime numbers occur less often, and they are more difficult to detect. The question naturally arose, "Is there a largest prime number?"

Euclid tackled this problem. He believed that prime numbers went on endlessly. A large prime number would always be topped by a larger one, he thought. Yet, all of his proofs fell short of showing that primes were infinite in number.

Success came when he took an unusual step. He assumed that a largest prime number did exist. Then he showed how it and the primes below it could be used to make a still larger prime number. If he found the largest prime, then a still larger one had to exist! Clearly, something was amiss. This dizzy contradiction proved his original assumption had to be wrong. There was no largest prime. Mathematicians today often employ this neat trick. They assume the opposite of what they think is true and then see if it leads to a ridiculous conclusion.

For generations, prime numbers appeared to have no particular practical use. Then, when computers sent data such as banking records over the Internet, people realized the data needed to be encrypted. Encrypted data is in a code that can only be read by the sender and receiver. To prevent a dishonest person from breaking the code, the secret transmission is based on very large prime numbers. Prime numbers have an important use after all.

Mathematicians used computers to test large numbers to see if they were prime. The largest prime number known at the beginning of the year 2000 had more than two million digits. To write it out would take a strip of paper more than three miles long.

Euclid also studied optics. Optics is the study of light. Light rays travel in a straight line except when they reflect from a surface or enter glass or water. Euclid's book on optics was particularly useful for artists. His tracing of light rays showed them how to draw three-dimensional objects on the surface of two-dimensional paper.

One of Euclid's students was King Ptolemy himself, who came to learn geometry. Because of its strict rules of logic, many people find geometry to be a challenge. King Ptolemy was no exception.

The king asked, "Can't you make your subject easier to understand?"

Euclid promptly replied, "There is no royal road to geometry."

Searching for the basic building blocks of nature was one of the activities of the ancient Greeks. Thales, the most ancient of Greek philosophers, believed that water was the essential ingredient from which all other physical objects were made. Water could be a solid (ice), liquid (liquid water) and gas (water vapor that makes clouds). Other philosophers disagreed and instead said that everything was made of four basic building blocks — earth, water, air, and fire. They gave the name elements to these building blocks.

Euclid searched for the building blocks of geometry. He began with basic ideas. From the building blocks of first principles, he developed proofs for more complex ideas. He called his book *Elements of Geometry*.

Euclid could have merely collected everything known about the subject and put it together in any which way. This was a common practice during his day. Instead, he carefully organized the book. He started with a number of definitions and basic assumptions. He arranged the rest of the book to follow logically. He supplied missing proofs. He wrote in a style that was remarkably clear.

The result was vastly superior to anything then in existence. All other books on geometry fell aside. When a person

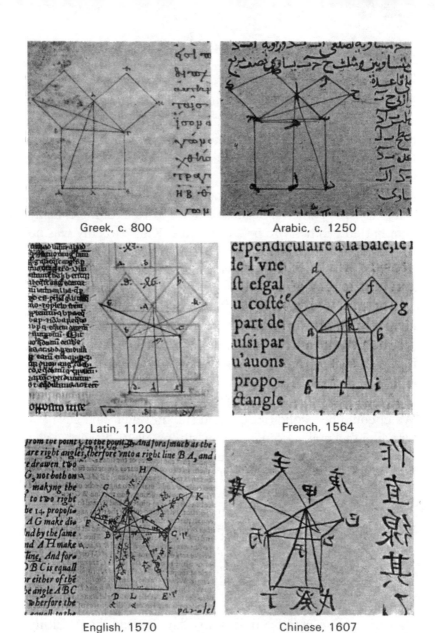

Greek, c. 800

Arabic, c. 1250

Latin, 1120

French, 1564

English, 1570

Chinese, 1607

A globe-girdling theorem: The Pythagorean theorem, first expounded more than 2,000 years ago, was familiar all over the civilized world by the 17th century. At top left of the grouping is a Greek text of Euclid's proof, and with it five translations. Although the Chinese text is only 350 years old, the Chinese were actually familiary with the theorem at about the time of Pythagoras.

said "geometry," everyone understood the person meant Euclid's geometry. Euclid taught more than geometry. His book was an introduction to logical thought. It showed how to develop a mathematical proof.

He also wrote books on astronomy, music, and other subjects. None of these books exist. They have become lost. We know of their existence only because students took notes from them. Early in the 1900s archaeologists uncovered one set of notes 500 miles from Alexandria on Elephantine Island in the Nile River. Perhaps the student had gone to that quiet location so he could think more clearly while he studied Euclid's books. The notes survived the years, but not the books.

Euclid's *Elements of Geometry* came close to being lost, too. Euclid wrote his books in Greek. After his death, Alexandria fell into Roman hands. Then in A.D. 640, Arab armies overran the city. They burned the museum and carted away the books. The Arabs advanced as far north as Spain. The Arabs translated Euclid's *Elements* into Arabic. The original Greek copies disappeared. In the 1100s, a traveler to Spain found an Arabic copy and translated it into Latin, the language of scholars in Europe.

In the late 1400s, *Elements of Geometry* was printed with the newly invented printing press. The book found a whole new audience. Euclid's treatment of geometry had a tremendous effect on the champions of scientific discovery such as Copernicus, Galileo, and Isaac Newton.

What made his book so important? For more than two thousand years, the book's structure has fascinated scientists. All geometric rules flowed from the definitions and basic assumptions that Euclid listed at the beginning. To these building blocks, he gave the name postulates. For instance, one of his postulates was that the shortest distance between two points is a straight line.

Another assumption was the parallel postulate. Lines are parallel if they run side by side forever without crossing one another. An example would be perfectly straight railroad tracks that run alongside one another endlessly. Suppose you have a straight line and a point above or below the line. How many straight lines can you draw through the point that are parallel to the first line? Euclid stated that only one line could be so drawn. The parallel postulate states: Through a point not on a given line, one and only one line can be drawn parallel to the given line.

Many people thought the parallel postulate was so obvious that it was a fact, and not an assumption. Modern astronomers realize now that powerful gravity fields can distort space. In the neighborhood of neutron stars and black holes, parallel lines may be impossible. All lines may intersect. Mathematicians realize that Euclid was correct in listing the parallel postulate as one of his assumptions.

Euclid's *Elements* are still taught in school. Although *Elements* is about geometry, what it teaches is how to think and reason. Modern science owes much to Euclid. Gathering facts alone is not science. Facts must be organized, summarized, and given logical order. People like Galileo, Isaac Newton, Albert Einstein, and scientists of today face a bewildering array of assumptions and observations. Euclid taught how to separate facts from assumptions. From *Elements*, scientists learn how to apply reasoning to facts and build general principles.

3

THE SAND RECKONER

The next great mathematician after Euclid was Archimedes. Far more is known about Archimedes than Euclid or any of the other ancient Greek scientists. We know, for instance, that his father's name was Phidias and that his father was an astronomer.

Archimedes studied in Alexandria in Egypt. His instructor was one of the teachers that Euclid trained. Some of Archimedes' letters to a friend in Alexandria still exist.

After spending some time in Egypt, Archimedes returned to his home of Syracuse on the island of Sicily. Hieron II ruled Syracuse. He saw Archimedes' genius and gave the great scientist whatever assistance he needed. Archimedes did not have to work or even teach, so he could devote his full time to studying science and mathematics. Archimedes made many useful inventions and discovered important scientific truths. This chapter will explore his mathematical discoveries.

Archimedes was always thinking and always drawing figures. On warm days, he would walk along the beach. He would stop and draw diagrams in the sand to help him understand difficult problems. On colder days, he would sit by the fire. If he needed to write, he would use a stick to rake out a layer of ash from the fire. He would draw figures in the ash. The Greeks took baths, and afterward anointed their bodies with olive oil. Archimedes would sometimes become lost in thought and trace out figures in the olive oil on his belly.

Archimedes calculated pi, π, to an accuracy never before achieved. Pi is the number given by dividing the circumference of a circle by its diameter. The circumference is the distance around a circle. The diameter is the distance across the circle through its center. Because of the curve of a circle, it is difficult to calculate its circumference exactly. Even Archimedes could not do the calculation to his satisfaction.

If the direct approach failed, Archimedes tried another way. He attacked a scientific challenge as if in a battle and would grasp any weapon to overcome the problem.

He found a way around the circle problem by working with figures that had straight sides. A regular polygon has sides that are straight lines and equal in length. A square is an example of a regular polygon. A square has four sides. A pentagon is a polygon of five sides. The more sides a polygon has, the more nearly it matches the shape of a circle. Finding the distance around a polygon is easier than finding the distance around a circle.

Archimedes

Archimedes put a 96-sided polygon inside a circle. He calculated the polygon's circumference divided by diameter to be 223/71, or about 3.1408. He then put a slightly bigger 96-sided polygon outside the circle. He calculated its circumference divided by its diameter to be 22/7, or about 3.1429. He had trapped pi between 223/71 and 22/7. He announced that the value of pi for a circle lay between the two numbers 22/7 and 223/71. The modern value for pi to four decimal places is 3.1416, which is between the two values Archimedes calculated.

It was the best value achieved by ancient mathematicians. Although other mathematicians improved on his answer, they still used his method of polygons to obtain a more accurate value. Almost two thousands years passed before anyone found a better way to make the calculation.

Archimedes also developed a mathematical trick to replace hard problems with a series of easier ones. For instance, Greeks knew how to measure the area, or enclosed space, of ordinary figures such as rectangles. What of odd-shaped figures with curving sides? How do you calculate their areas? Archimedes found a solution. He mathematically cut the figure into a series of strips. Each strip was a long skinny rectangle. Although the ends of the rectangles might be misshapen, if the original figure were cut into enough rectangles, the error would become so small it did not matter.

One of the greatest irritations to Archimedes was the lack of a good way to represent numbers. The Greeks and Romans used letters to stand for numbers. In the Roman system, I stood for one, V for five, X for ten, L for fifty, C for one hundred and M for one thousand. The Romans wrote the number 1223 as MCCXXIII. Multiplying and dividing with Roman numerals was especially difficult. To show numbers much beyond one thousand, M, was not easily done.

The location of the symbol did not change its value. If we write 23, that is different from 32. The Greeks and Romans ignored position. XXIII was 10 + 10 + 1 + 1 + 1 = 23. If they wrote it as IIIXX it was still 1 + 1 + 1 + 10 + 10 = 23. Later, a slight change was made in Roman numerals so that a smaller number before a larger number was subtracted from the larger number. For instance, VI was 5 + 1 = 6, but IV was 5 -1 = 4. This made Roman numerals even more confusing.

Archimedes once heard a person use the expression "As countless as the grains of sand on the seashore." As he thought about this statement, Archimedes realized that it was incorrect. Unlike prime numbers that go on endlessly, the number of sand particles do have an end. Their numbers are not infinite. Could he come up with a number so large it had to exceed the number of grains of sand?

As he thought about his, he developed his own numbering system. He told about his ideas in his book *The Sand Reckoner*. He addressed the book to Gelon, the son of King Hieron. He wrote in a simple language that Gelon could understand. Archimedes invented the name myriad for 10,000. It is ten multiplied by itself four times: $10 * 10 * 10 * 10 = 10,000$. He made a still larger number as a myriad myriad, or one hundred million (100,000,000.) He called this number an octade. It is ten, multiplied by itself eight times. Octade means eight. A still larger number would be an octade octade (10,000,000,000,000,000.)

Although the number of grains of sand was immense, he could name their number with his counting system.

The last days of Archimedes are described by Plutarch, a Greek historian. He wrote a biography of the Roman general Marcus Claudis Marcellius. Known as the Sword of Rome, Marcellius laid siege to Syracuse during the Second Punic War. With Archimedes' help, the people of Syracuse kept the Romans from storming the city for three years. Finally, however, the Romans prevailed. Marcellus left strict orders for the life of Archimedes to be spared.

A Roman soldier came across a 76-year-old man drawing diagrams in the sand on the beach. He ordered the man to move along. Instead, the man scolded the warrior. "Soldier, stand away from my diagrams!"

According to Plutarch, the soldier killed the man with a sword, not knowing that he taken the life of the great Archimedes.

4

MATHEMATICS IN ECLIPSE

The Romans took Archimedes' island of Syracuse and the rest of the empire once held by the Greeks. The Romans put Greek discoveries to work. They built roads for their chariots, aqueducts to carry water, and ships to sail the Mediterranean. They dug canals and tunnels and made many great engineering feats. But they made few new discoveries of their own.

In the 400s, the Roman Empire began to collapse. With the fall of Rome in A.D. 476 and the destruction of Alexandria by the Arabs in 642, the Golden Age in Europe ended. Governments crumbled. Learning went into decline. Education became of little importance and few people could read or write. Most people in Europe lived as farmers and worked on land they did not own. They were hardly more than slaves on minor kingdoms known as serfdoms.

The rest of the world continued to make advances. The Mayan culture in South America, the Chinese in the Orient, the Arabs in the Middle East, and others did not fall into a decline. Historians prefer to use the term Middle Ages for this period. For people in Europe, a far bleaker description is appropriate. To them, the period was the Dark Ages.

During the 1100s, a group of merchants did begin trade

again. They lived in Italy, in cities such as Venice, Florence, and Pisa. They carried out a trade in sugar, spices, and silk that came from Arab caravans along the historic Silk Road from China.

Guilielmo Bonacci was an official of Pisa, a town in central Italy. His son, Leonardo Fibonacci, was born in 1170. The *Fi* in front of Bonacci is a way of writing "son of Bonacci."

Pisa was one of the few cities to survive the collapse of the Roman Empire. The city had a fine church of dazzling white marble with rich decorations. When Fibonacci was four years old, construction began for a bell tower of the church. The builders soon realized their original calculations for construction were in error. The tower had a shallow foundation and it would not stand upright in the soft soil. It began tilting to one side. The Leaning Tower of Pisa became a tourist attraction almost as soon as it was finished.

When Fibonacci was 20 years old, he became a trade representative like his father. He traveled to Egypt, Syria, Greece, and Sicily. He, like so many merchants, struggled with making arithmetic calculations. He had to convert weights and measures from one system to another, calculate the rate of exchange for money, divide profit and expenses among partners, and calculate the percentages of taxes and figure interest. Doing this with Roman numerals was a real headache.

Everywhere he traveled, he watched merchants make their calculations. He learned number tricks to make his work easier. While in Algeria in Northern Africa, he discovered an entirely new way of doing math. The Moors were the people of North Africa who had taken on the customs of the Arabs and married into their families. They had learned the new math from Arabs who had visited India.

The Moors taught Fibonacci the new numbering system and how to calculate with it. Fibonacci was astonished at the ease of doing math with the new system.

He saw the two key features that made it superior to Roman numerals. First, it was a place value system. A place value system allows a symbol to change in value depending on where it is located in a number. For instance, 5,358 has two 5s in it. The 5 on the left stands for 5,000. The 5 in the middle stands for 50. The second key feature was the use of a new numeral, 0. The invention of zero, 0, made place value possible. Suppose the number was 303. Without a

Leonardo Fibonacci

zero, it would be written as 33, which is incorrect. But with the zero, 303 can be correctly written.

Fibonacci realized that all of mathematics changed with the invention of the numeral 0. With just ten digits — 0, 1, 2, 3, 4, 5, 6, 7, 8, 9 — a person could easily write numbers from 0 to far beyond the myriad myriad of Archimedes. The invention of place value and the numeral zero were great achievements that completely escaped the great Greek minds.

Fibonacci could hardly wait to return to Pisa and show others the advantages of the new system. At Pisa he wrote several books about the system. The best known one was *Book of Calculating*. In it, he showed step by step how to use the new math. Fibonacci began with rules for adding numbers, subtracting, multiplying, and dividing. He gave examples and showed how to work common problems that came up in everyday business.

He is best remembered for a simple puzzle that can be stated like this: After becoming two months old, a female rabbit gives birth to exactly one female rabbit every month. At age two months, the second rabbit gives birth to another female rabbit and does so every month thereafter. When the third rabbit is two months old, she begins giving birth to a single female rabbit every month, and so on. Assume no rabbits escape and none die. Fibonacci asked, "How many rabbits will there be at the end of each month for a year?"

In the first month, there is but one rabbit. The second month there is still only one rabbit. In the third month, she gives birth so there are two rabbits. The fourth month she gives birth again so there are three rabbits. On the fifth month both she and her first daughter give birth, so there are a total now of five rabbits. In the sixth month, she continues to give birth, her daughter continues to give birth and now her granddaughter gives birth. The rabbits number eight.

The number of rabbits for each month is: 1, 1, 2, 3, 5, 8, and so on. Rather than thinking of rabbits, look at the numbers. Starting with 2, any number in the series is equal to the sum of the previous two numbers. What comes after eight? Add five and eight: $5 + 8 = 13$. What comes after 13? Add 8 and 13: $8 + 13 = 21$. The next four numbers in the series are 34, 55, 89, and 144. At the end of 12 months, there will be 144 rabbits.

People began sending Leonardo Fibonacci difficult problems and mathematical riddles to solve, which he did. Some people took up mathematics as a hobby. They enjoyed the sheer fun of solving riddles. Today Leonard Fibonacci is well known among amateur mathematicians because of his multiplying rabbit riddle. The numbers 1, 1, 2, 3, 5, 8, 13, 21, 34, and so on are known as the Fibonacci series.

Why is the string of numbers so interesting? In addition to having many surprising mathematical properties, they are found in nature in unexpected places. As scientists investigated the world, the Fibonacci numbers came up time and again. For instance, the chambered nautilus, a marine creature, has a spiral-shaped shell. The chambers in the shell follow a design given by Fibonacci numbers.

The number of petals on some flowers is always a Fibonacci number. For instance, buttercups have 5 petals, black-eyed Susans have 21 petals and plantain has 34. All of these are Fibonacci numbers. The seed head of a large sunflower has the seeds arranged in a spiral shape. The number of spirals is always a Fibonacci number. Some pinecones also show the spirals.

Leonardo Fibonacci's real accomplishment was not the rabbit riddle, but his *Book of Calculating*. His examples convinced others to begin using place value. Its ease of use attracted bankers, businessmen, surveyors, engineers, astronomers, and scientists. Fibonacci's methods reduced the chances for mistakes.

During the Middle Ages, calculations in math and science often did not agree with the real world. Planets did not quite follow their assigned orbit, cannonballs did not follow their predicted path, and towers such as the Leaning Tower of Pisa were not as stable as the designers would have wished.

Usually, when problems occurred, critics blamed the mathematicians for making the errors.

However, with the place value system, calculating mistakes became far less common. Mathematicians realized the errors were not in their calculations. The errors were in how scientists understood nature. Most of what was known about the natural world come through translations of ancient Greek texts. The books were full of errors. Scientists began questioning the Greek ideas about the natural world.

Fibonacci made the place value system for numbers popular in Europe. He set the stage for a reawakening of learning that helped end the Dark Ages.

5

ON THE SHOULDERS OF GIANTS

I saac Newton was born in England on a cold Christmas Day in 1642. He was undersized and weak. His mother was afraid he would not live through the winter. However, Isaac survived the harsh winter and grew into a healthy child.

His father, who could not read or write, died three months before Isaac was born. His mother was poor. She lived in an old manor house and had some farmland. The building was in disrepair and the farmland poorly managed. After struggling to run the farm on her own, Isaac's mother married Barnabas Smith. He was a minister of the gospel at the nearby parish of North Witham.

She moved away to live with her husband. Isaac remained behind on the farm with his grandmother. The steeple of the church where his stepfather preached was visible from the manor. When he grew older, he would walk across the fields to visit his mother. He used the steeple as a guide to his destination.

He grew up during the dark days of the English Civil War. Because of the fighting, his mother warned him to hide behind the hedges if he saw soldiers. Oliver Cromwell and the parliamentary forces prevailed in fighting against King Charles I.

Cromwell took the title Lord Protector, rather than king. He ruled the three nations of England, Scotland, and Ireland.

In 1653, Isaac's mother moved back home because Barnabas Smith died. She brought his large collection of books about the Bible with her. Isaac was astonished that 200 books could be devoted to a single subject. It impressed him that the Bible must be an important book worthy of study. He built a bookshelf for the collection, using planks from packing crates. He spent hours reading the books. Throughout his life, he devoted more time to studying Bible subjects than he did mathematics or science.

Isaac's study of the Bible gave him comfort during difficult times. He read it through often.

Isaac Newton spent only a short time at home with his mother. He was sent away to attend school at Grantham. He lived in an upstairs apartment with the Clark family. Mr. Clark was a druggist who had his shop below the apartment. He also had a library of books on scientific subjects. Isaac explored chemistry and science with the books.

Isaac also bought books of his own, including John Bate's *Mysteries of Nature and Art.* The book soon became one of his favorites. It included plans for mechanical models. The young Isaac Newton enjoyed making wooden models of clocks, wagons, and windmills. He used his skill at mathematics to measure the parts so the models would be to scale.

His models worked. The clock kept time by dripping water into a container. A stick marked off in hours floated in the lower container. As the stick floated higher, it showed the passage of hours. The wheels turned on his wagons, doors opened on the windmill, and sails spun. He made a miniature flourmill with a grindstone turned by the force of the wind.

Isaac also made tiny lanterns of crinkled paper with a candle inside. On dark winter mornings the lanterns lighted his way to school. At school, Isaac made his best grades in Bible class.

The school taught only the basics of arithmetic. Isaac found books on geometry and algebra and studied the subjects on his own. Because he ignored formal assignments, his grades were no better than the grades of the other students. No one could guess that he would grow up to be the greatest scientist who ever lived.

In fact, no one could figure that he would achieve an exceptional success at anything. He certainly was not suited to being a farmer. After graduation, he came home to train to manage his mother's farm. Once, he was leading a horse back to the barn. The horse slipped free of its bridle. Isaac, lost in thought, continued home, dragging the reins with the empty bridle behind him. When sent to the meadow to attend to the sheep, he instead became busy calculating the size of the field while the sheep strayed away.

On market day, he would take the produce to Grantham to sell. Often, he would leave the business dealings in the hands of a trusted hired hand. Isaac would visit the Clark family where he had boarded. Instead of learning the skill of buying and selling, he would spend the day happily reading books in the Clark's library.

In 1658, a terrible storm blew across the country. It uprooted old trees. Isaac ran outside to make sure that the barn doors were closed with the animals safely inside. On the way back, he spent a few minutes jumping with the wind and then jumping against it. He experienced firsthand the invisible force of the wind.

His mother talked with her brother about Isaac's future. Her brother, William Ayscough, was also a preacher of the gospel. He had attended Cambridge University. William suggested that Isaac go to college while he searched for a suitable profession.

Unfortunately, Isaac and his mother did not have the money for tuition, but Isaac found a way. He paid for his room and meals by doing chores for his professors. He polished shoes, delivered messages, ran errands, and served the professors their meals. Isaac studied theology and mathematics at Cambridge.

He graduated in 1665 with no particular notice. He still did not have a profession, so he decided to stay on as a fellow. A fellow could study advanced courses, and the school provided room and meals. Maybe later a teaching job would open. Isaac's favorite teacher was Professor Barlow, who taught mathematics. Professor Barlow was a forceful speaker and great scientist who gave God credit for his success. Professor Barlow said, "God is the creator of all things, even success."

In 1665, terrible news interrupted Isaac's schooling. The Black Death, bubonic plague, struck London. During the hot summer, ten thousand people died each month. No one knew the cause or the cure. The disease struck most fiercely in places where people lived close together. The Black Death spread to Cambridge. University officials closed the school as a safety measure. Students scattered to the countryside away from the epidemic.

Isaac Newton escaped to his mother's farm in the country. In good weather, he worked at a study table in the apple orchard.

Isaac explored a dozen different subjects, including light, astronomy, mathematics, chemistry, and physics. When he tired of one subject, he switched to some other unsolved puzzle of science.

Raising a binomial to a power was one of the problems in mathematics that captured his attention. The word binomial was from "bi," meaning two, and "nomial," meaning names. A binomial was an expression in algebra made of two numbers. Mathematicians showed it as $a + b$, with the letter a standing for one number and b standing for the other number.

Binomials could be added, subtracted, multiplied, divided, and raised to powers like other numbers. However, raising a binomial to a power was difficult because it expanded into a series of complicated terms. The simplest binomial raised to a power was $(a + b)^2$. The superscript 2 showed to multiple $a + b$ by itself: $(a + b) * (a + b)$. The * means to multiply. Isaac carried out the multiplication and gave the answer as $1a^2 + 2ab + 1b^2$.

What about $(a + b)^3$? When multiplied out the answer was: $(a + b) * (a + b) * (a + b) = 1a^3 + 3a^2b + 3ab^2 + 1b^3$. As the powers increased, the expression became more tangled. When Isaac multiplied out a binomial raised to the fourth power, it had five terms: $(a + b)^4 = 1a^4 + 4a^3b + 6a^2b^2 + 4a^2b^3 + 1b^4$.

As he pored over the calculations, Isaac saw a pattern emerge. He discovered he could calculate the terms in his head. For instance, the number in front of the second term was always the power to which the binomial was raised. Isaac worked out his solution in the language of mathematics and sent it to Professor Barlow at Cambridge.

Professor Barlow pronounced Isaac's discovery of the binomial theorem to be worthy of a first-rate mathematician. He encouraged Isaac to use his vacation to continue his scientific studies.

Although Isaac always looked for the easy way to solve a problem, he never let the difficulty of a task prevent him from tackling an idea. Sometimes he would go for days keeping a problem in his head. He would fill page after page with calculations.

He gave himself difficult tasks such as figuring the area under curves. The ancient Greeks were interested in four curves — circle, ellipse, parabola, and hyperbola — that could be formed by cutting a cone in various directions. If a cone is cut parallel to the base, the result is a circle. If the cut is at an angle to the base, then the result is an ellipse.

The ancient Greeks found ways to calculate the area of circles and ellipses. However, for more complicated figures, calculating the areas was too difficult.

Isaac sometimes took long rides on his horse as he thought about problems. One day he came across an ancient manor house with a great curving archway. He measured the arch and tried to calculate the area of the opening.

Like Archimedes, he broke the difficult problem into a series of easier ones. Isaac replaced the area under the arch with several rectangles that covered the shape of the arch. As

Though a mathematical genius, Isaac Newton devoted much of his life to theological study and, in later years to his job as master of the mint. He developed his version of calculus in 1665 but did not publish his findings until 1704.

Isaac divided the arch into more and more rectangles, they became smaller and smaller.

Isaac wondered if he could sum an infinite number of vanishingly small rectangles. Would the result give a meaningful answer? It seemed a contradiction. On the one hand, the number of rectangles increased without number. On the other hand, the size of the rectangles became so small their areas became practically zero.

Isaac Newton invented what he called "fluxions." The word was from Latin meaning to flow. His flowing math allowed him to find the sum of an infinite number of rectangles, each with an area approaching zero. To Isaac, it was merely a neat solution to an interesting problem. He did not realize he had made one of the greatest mathematical discoveries of all time. Later, he developed fluxions into a powerful mathematical tool that became known as calculus.

Scientists solved difficult problems with calculus. Astronomers calculated the orbit of comets and predicted their return. For the first time, ordinary mathematicians could do calculations that had baffled the Greeks.

Later scientists applied calculus to problems in biology, medicine, and nuclear physics. Biologists tracked the speed at which a swarm of germs in a colony multiplied. Chemists computed the rate that millions of atoms combined during a chemical reaction. Nuclear engineers predicted the energy released by billions of radioactive atoms in uranium.

When Isaac tired of his mathematical calculations, he switched to other riddles. Scientists argued about the source of the colored bands in the rainbow. Most scientists believed sunlight was pure. They claimed that the pure light of the sun became tainted with colors by passing through raindrops.

Isaac attended a local fair and bought some glass prisms. The prisms separated the rays of sunlight into the colors of the rainbow. Scientists assumed the colors came from the glass.

Isaac proved that the colors were present in the sunlight all along. Sunlight was not pure white light. Instead, it was a mixture of all of the colors. Raindrops and the glass prisms separated the colors and made them visible.

He studied the work of Galileo who had investigated motion of heavy metal balls on earth. Galileo experimented with the speed of rolling balls going across a flat table. Galileo concluded that a ball would roll in a straight line at a constant speed on a flat surface. To change its direction or speed, a force had to act on it. The ball slowed because of air resistance and friction with the table.

If the ball rolled off the end of the table, then it would change direction. It fell toward the center of the earth. The ball fell faster and faster each second. Galileo's experiments with falling objects showed they gained speed at the rate of 32 feet per second every second. At the end of one second, a falling ball traveled at 32 feet per second toward the surface of the earth. At the end of two seconds, it fell at 64 feet per second. Its speed continued to increase until it struck the earth.

The German scientist Johannes Kepler studied motions in the heavens. He showed that the moon and planets traveled in closed orbits at nearly constant speed. The moon, for instance, orbited the earth in an elliptical orbit. An ellipse had a shape similar to a slightly flattened circle.

One day while working at his study table in the apple orchard, Isaac Newton began thinking about the discoveries of Galileo and Kepler. Galileo had shown that an apple would fall to earth in a straight line but it constantly changed speed. Kepler had shown that the moon traveled around the earth at a nearly constant speed but constantly changed direction.

Why the difference? Scientists in Newton's day believed that forces in the heavens were different from forces on earth. The force of gravity acted on the apple. An entirely different force acted on the moon. Scientists claimed that the earth produced a whirlpool effect that gave the moon its motion.

Isaac Newton wondered if perhaps the apple and the moon responded to the same force of gravity. Could the force of gravity that pulled the apple from the tree also extend out into space and bend the moon's path into a curve? What would be its strength?

The apple was 4,000 miles from the center of the earth. The moon was 240,000 miles from the center of the earth. Isaac's calculations showed that the moon was 60 times farther away than the apple: 240,000/4,000 = 60. Would gravity acting on the moon be 60 times weaker?

No, it was far weaker. Isaac calculated the force needed to change the straight-line motion of the moon into a curved orbit. When he compared it with the apple, he found that the apple received a force 3,600 times as great. Isaac saw that $3,600 = 60 * 60 = 60^2$. This led him to the important conclusion that the force of gravity decreases by the square of the distance.

Isaac showed that earth's gravity extends far out into space and controls the moon in its orbit. He believed that the sun's gravity acted in the same way on the planets.

During his 18 months on the farm, Isaac gained insights into science that would be useful to him throughout his career. He called 1666 his marvelous year.

After the Black Death ran its course, Isaac Newton returned to Cambridge. He graduated in 1668 without a permanent job. Although he had made many important discoveries, he had published only a few of them. He was still practically unknown.

Professor Barlow did recognize Isaac's genius. Professor Barlow resigned from his teaching position at Cambridge. With Professor Barlow's support, Isaac was appointed to the vacancy. Isaac now received a salary for doing what he loved — investigating mathematics and science. He spent the next 20 years at Cambridge.

He perfected what he had learned during his forced vacation on the farm. In the 1680s, scientists still argued about whether gravity grew weaker by the square of the distance or not. In 1684 a young astronomer, Edmund Halley, visited Newton and asked his opinion on the subject.

Isaac Newton promptly replied that gravity decreased by the square of the distance.

"How do you know?" Halley asked.

"Why, I have calculated it," Isaac Newton explained.

When Halley learned more about Newton's law of gravity, he insisted that Newton make it available to astronomers.

For about 18 months Isaac worked on the book. He called it *Principia Mathematica*. In the first section he stated the three laws of motions and the law of gravity. In the second part he calculated the masses of the sun and planets and found their distances. The third part took up tides and showed they were caused primarily by the gravitational attraction of the sun and moon. He also showed how to calculate the paths of comets.

Until then, comets with their long glowing tails were one of the most mysterious objects in the solar system. Newton showed they obeyed the law of gravity like the planets. Edmund Halley applied Newton's methods to predict the return of a particular comet. When his calculations proved correct, the comet was named Halley's Comet in his honor.

One illustration in *Principia* showed a powerful cannon on a mountaintop high above the atmosphere. If the cannon were powerful enough, it could shoot a cannonball all the way around the earth. The cannonball would be above the friction of the earth's atmosphere. It would continue circling the earth forever. Isaac Newton was the first to suggest that an artificial satellite could be put in orbit around the earth.

Scientists hailed *Principia* as the greatest scientific work ever published.

The law of gravity became Isaac Newton's best-known and most important discovery. The law states: The force of attraction between any two bodies in the universe is directly proportional to the product of their masses and inversely proportional to the square of the distance separating their centers.

Isaac warned against viewing the universe as only some machine like a great clock. He said, "Gravity explains the motions of the planets, but it cannot explain who set the planets in motion. God governs all things, and knows all that is or can be done."

As the years passed, people came to understand the importance of his discoveries. Isaac received many honors. In 1705, Queen Anne knighted him Sir Isaac Newton. It was the first knighthood for scientific discoveries. Isaac Newton died in 1727. He was buried in Westminster Abbey in a plot reserved for a king.

Despite his fame as a scientist, the Bible and not nature had been Isaac Newton's greatest passion. He wrote two books about the Bible. He devoted more time to Scripture than to science. He said, "I have a fundamental belief in the Bible as the Word of God, written by men who were inspired. I study the Bible daily."

Many people had assisted Isaac Newton in his success. These people included Edmund Halley, Professor Barlow, Galileo, and Johannes Kepler. Isaac Newton saw that he had built on the advances of others. He said, "If I have seen farther, it is by standing on the shoulders of giants."

6

A FAMILY OF MATHEMATICIANS

The Bible says, "Whoever has will be given more, and he will have an abundance" (Matt. 13:12). Jesus was speaking of spiritual matters. Scientists call this statement Matthew's law and apply it to the way certain locations attract great scientists. Once a university earns a good reputation, bright students flock there and enhance its appeal even more.

In ancient Greece, Athens earned the reputation as the center of learning. Socrates, Plato, and Aristotle lived in Athens. The city attracted students who wanted to study under the great thinkers of that age.

Later, Alexandria rose to the center of learning. Euclid, Archimedes, Eratosthenes, and others made it the powerhouse of mathematics and astronomy. Informed students abandoned Athens in favor of Alexandria.

Following the Dark Ages, cities in Italy rose to prominence. In the 1500s, Florence became a center for artists. Leonardo da Vinca studied and painted there. Pisa, Italy, had its share of great scientists who helped the revival of learning in Europe. Marcello Malpighi taught medicine at the University of Pisa. He discovered the tiny capillary blood vessels that connected arteries to veins.

Galileo studied at the University of Pisa. To prove his

contention that all objects fall at the same speed, he was rumored to have dropped two balls of different weights from the Leaning Tower of Pisa. Later, Galileo taught at the University of Padua, another Italian city.

In the 1600s, the scene shifted to England. The chemist Robert Boyle, his assistant Robert Hooke, architect Christopher Wren, astronomer Edmund Halley, and Isaac Newton made London, with its Royal Society, the chief city for scientific discoveries. For almost one hundred years scientists visited London to learn the latest advances.

In the 1700s, Basel, a university town in Switzerland took the lead. Sometimes it is difficult to know why one town becomes the center of learning. In the case of Basel, the reason is easy to understand. The success of Basel can be traced to a single family — the Bernoullis.

Nicolaus Bernoulli came to Switzerland because of its greater religious freedom. He became a wealthy merchant. He had three sons: Jacob, Nicolaus, and Johann. He assumed his first son, Jacob, would become a businessman, too. Instead, Jacob mastered calculus on his own and made improvements to it. He taught calculus at the University in Basel, Switzerland.

Calculus makes it possible to study bodies that have two motions at once. For instance, suppose a wagon wheel is rolling forward. A point on the wheel has two motions — the forward motion of the wagon and a circular motion as the wheel rotates. What curve does the point on the wheel trace out? The curve is called a cycloid, which Jacob investigated with calculus.

For practical applications, mathematicians were interested in figuring the highest, lowest, shortest, or fastest. Suppose a farmer wanted to build a sheep pen, but had only enough stone to make one with a certain perimeter (distance around). What shape should it have to enclose the most space? Should it be a triangle, rectangle, square, circle, or some other shape? The answer was a circle, and the Greeks knew the answer to this question.

A more complicated question involves speed and distance. Suppose a roller coaster traveled from a point at the top of the ride to a point farther down the ride. The shortest distance between the two points was a straight line. Would some other shape for the ramp cause the roller coaster car to travel between the two locations more rapidly? Suppose the ramp dropped down quickly and then curved toward its destination. The roller coaster car would fall sharply at first and gain speed to carry it quickly to the next point. A ramp with a sag in it was longer than a straight ramp. Would the faster speed make up for the longer distance? Yes, although the distance was greater, the car gained enough speed to make the trip more quickly.

Jacob Bernoulli

Jacob Bernoulli found the best shape for the fastest speed. The curve was the same type that was traced out by a point on a wagon wheel — a cycloid.

What shape did a rope take when it was held loosely at each end? Was it one of the curves investigated by the ancient Greeks? No, Jacob said. Although simple to produce, the curve was mathematically far more complicated. The shape of a loosely held rope was a catenary.

Jacob's study of catenary curves had real-world applications. Engineers knew that cables holding suspension bridges had the shape of a catenary. By knowing its exact form, they could build bridges that could carry heavier loads and span wider rivers.

Jacob studied spirals and noted that each segment mirrored the properties of the entire spiral. He directed that a spiral would be cut on his tombstone with the words, "Though changed I shall arise the same."

All three of Nicolaus Bernoulli's sons trained for different professions but ended up as mathematicians. The middle brother earned a degree as a lawyer. At first he taught law in Germany. Later he, too, became a professor of mathematics. Johann, Jacob's younger brother, studied to become a doctor. He earned a medical degree, but became a mathematician. When Jacob died, his mathematics position at Basel went to Johann.

Johann also had three sons. Mathematicians were not well paid. Despite being a mathematician himself, Johann insisted that his sons study some other profession. The first son, Nicolaus (named after his uncle and grandfather) avoided becoming a full-time mathematician. He did teach his younger brothers the subject.

The youngest brother was Johann II, named after his father. He became a teacher of language and grammar. However, when his father died, he took his father's post as instructor of mathematics at Basel. Johann had two sons. Both studied law, yet, after they received their degrees, they went on to scientific pursuits. One became an astronomer in Berlin, Germany, and the other taught mathematics at St. Petersburg.

The three generations of Bernoulli's produced eight world-class mathematicians.

7

A FATHER AND
SON TRAGEDY

P robably the most talented member of the Bernoulli family was Daniel Bernoulli, Johann's middle son. Each year the Paris Academy of Science gave a prize for the greatest scientific achievement in the previous year. To win the prize a single time was enough to make a scientific reputation. Daniel Bernoulli won the prize ten times!

Daniel Bernoulli became world famous while still a young man. When most people heard his name, they assumed he was an old and wise professor. While traveling, Daniel struck up a conversation with a stranger. When they introduced themselves, Daniel said, "I am Daniel Bernoulli."

In disbelief, the stranger said sarcastically, "And I am Isaac Newton."

When Daniel was growing up, his father wanted him to pursue a career in business. Instead, Daniel decided to become a doctor. His father took comfort that Daniel had rejected mathematical pursuits.

Daniel studied medicine at Basel. As part of his degree, the university required that he write a medical research paper. Daniel decided to investigate airflow in the lungs. To correctly explain the action of the lungs required that he apply mathematics to the motion of fluids. A fluid is any substance that flows. Water and air are two examples of fluids.

Daniel wondered if the physics that Newton developed also applied to fluids such as water and air. Until then, scientists had applied Newton's laws of motion to large, solid objects such as pendulums, projectiles, the moon, and planets.

In the cold winters around Basel, Daniel had seen the three laws of motion demonstrated by ice skaters on the frozen rivers and lakes. A skater who got up to speed could effortlessly glide across the frozen surface of the lake. Because the friction was reduced to a minimum, the skater enjoyed the results of the first law. Once in motion, additional force did not need to be applied. Newton's first law stated that a body at rest will remain at rest and a body in motion will remain in constant straight-line motion unless an outside force acts on it.

To change direction or speed, however, did require force. The amount of force depended on the mass. A draft horse pulled a sled loaded with firewood. At first, the horse had to labor to get the sled moving. His nostrils flared and filled the air with his frosty breath. His hooves pawed at the frozen ground as he struggled to pull the sled. A team of horses provided more force and got the heavy sled moving more quickly than a single horse. A lightly loaded sled was more easily moved than a heavy one. The second law stated that the change in speed of a body was directly proportional to the force but inversely proportional to the mass.

A mother and daughter stood motionless in the middle of the frozen lake. The mother pushed on the daughter to get her moving. The daughter glided away in one direction. The mother glided away in the other direction. They exerted opposite forces upon one another in keeping with the third law. The third law of motion stated that for every action force there is an opposite reaction force.

Did blood in the arteries and air in the lungs also follow the three laws of motion? Did the rules that apply to large solid objects also apply to fluids? Daniel asked his father this question. His father thought so but had been unable to prove it. Even the great Isaac Newton had been unable to apply his rules to the way that fluids moved.

After graduation from Basel, Daniel applied for a teaching post at the university. However, nothing was open. Rather than remaining idle, he traveled to Italy where he took advanced courses in medicine at the University of Padua.

While at Padua, Daniel studied the circulation of blood. About 75 years earlier, William Harvey discovered that the heart pumped blood throughout the body in a closed path. Although an Englishman, William Harvey traveled to Italy and enrolled at the University of Padua. It was considered the best medical school in the world. Galileo taught at Padua while Harvey was there.

Daniel carefully studied Harvey's book *On the Motion of the Heart and Blood*. Daniel was impressed with Harvey's clear writing and careful experiments to prove his case. Daniel realized that blood followed the same physical laws as other solid objects.

Daniel's study of blood was interrupted by illness. As he recovered, he occupied his mind by designing an improved hourglass. He selected that problem because it was simple and did not require great effort. An hourglass measured time as sand trickled through a narrow neck from an upper glass chamber into a similar glass chamber on bottom.

Daniel designed an hourglass that could be used aboard a ship. Measuring short periods of time aboard a ship pitching about on the ocean waves was difficult. Daniel's hourglass worked correctly even during a storm. He entered the design in a competition held by the French Academy. Much to his surprise, it captured first place in the competition.

While at Padua, a friend helped Daniel put together a book on mathematics titled *Some Mathematical Exercises*. He showed how to apply calculus to currents of flowing water. Despite his best efforts to please his father, Daniel's first book was one on mathematics. His father was not happy.

At age 25, Daniel returned to Basel, still without a job.

However, a letter was waiting for him from Empress Catherine I of Russia. Daniel knew that she had lived an interesting life. She had been born to a peasant family and became an orphan at age three. A Lutheran minister raised her. A Russian commander took her captive as a slave during one of the many battles. He sold her to a prince in the Russian court. Later, she became the wife of Peter the Great, ruler of all Russia.

When Peter the Great died, Catherine I became the ruler of Russia. Like her husband, she wanted to make Russia a more modern country. She believed an academy staffed by great scientists would strengthen the country. She invited Daniel to join the Imperial Academy in St. Petersburg.

Daniel was not too keen on traveling to Russia. His brother Nicolaus agreed to go with him. Catherine I found a position for Nicolaus, so the two brothers went to St. Petersburg in 1725. They roomed together. Unfortunately, after a year Nicolaus died.

Daniel made plans to come home. "I do not want to live alone in Russia," he wrote to his father.

Daniel's father insisted that he remain in Russia. Johann explained that nothing was open for Daniel in Switzerland. Johann promised to send a countryman as a roommate.

Johann had been favorably impressed with a young Swiss student who had come to Basel to study. The young genius was named Leonhard Euler. He arranged for Euler to go to St. Petersburg as assistant and roommate to Daniel.

With Euler, Daniel took up his study of the flow of fluids again. All thoughts of a medical practice disappeared as he immersed himself in the mathematics of fluids. Like so many in his family, he became a mathematician in spite of himself. He never became a practicing physician.

Daniel's exploration of fluids had a practical application. Peter the Great had been interested in shipbuilding. He encouraged the scientific design of ships. Daniel's discoveries found a ready audience with the Russian Navy. A smoothly flowing fluid does not take as much energy as one with eddies and currents. Ships with a shape that promote smooth flow cut through water more efficiently than those that create eddies and wakes. Daniel helped design hulls so ships sailed more efficiently. Better ships carried cargo at reduced cost. He also became the first to take a person's blood pressure. When doctors were called to help a sick person, they took the patient's temperature and measured the pulse rate. The pulse showed how fast the heart was beating. They did not take the blood pressure because they had no way to do so.

Because of his medical training, Daniel knew that blood pressure might indicate health problems in the human body. Low blood pressure might indicate poor circulation or explain why a patient was weak or tended to faint. High blood pressure could be dangerous, too. High pressure could cause blood vessels to burst.

Daniel invented a small device to measure the pressure of the blood that flowed in arteries. Doctors began using his invention to take the blood pressure of their patients.

Despite his success in Russia, Daniel did not particularly enjoy the harsh winters or serving Catherine I, who was a headstrong ruler. Each year, he begged his father to find him a place to teach in Basel.

"Nothing is here for you," his father said. "Stay in St. Petersburg."

In 1733, Leonhard Euler married and no longer roomed with Daniel. Daniel had been in Russia seven years and had enough. He learned of an opening as professor of plant science at Basel. He agreed to take the job to escape from Russia. Later, he became professor of physics, a position more to his liking.

Daniel became the first scientist to track energy changes when working with fluids. Energy is the ability to do work. Energy can be of two types, potential or active. Potential energy is stored energy. Water high behind a dam has potential energy. Once the water is released, it changes into active energy. Active energy is energy due to motion. Rushing water can turn a waterwheel to do the work of grinding grain.

A coiled spring has potential energy. When a coiled spring

is released, it gives active energy to a watch to turn the hands and keep time. Windup toys had potential energy in mainsprings. When the mainsprings were released, they turned wheels as active energy. Daniel realized that when potential energy is lost, an equal amount of active energy is gained. This is called the law of conservation of energy. He was the first to realize its importance.

A moving fluid such as air has active energy

Johann Bernoulli

from its motion. The faster the air flows, the greater is its active energy. Daniel realized air also had potential energy due to its pressure. Air under pressure was like a compressed spring. Energy was stored in pressurized air. The greater the pressure, the greater the potential energy.

Daniel wondered what happened to the pressure when the flow increased. Did its pressure increase or decrease? Because he knew that energy is conserved, Daniel had the answer. If air gains active energy due to motion, then it must lose potential energy due to pressure. If the speed of a fluid increases, then the pressure of the fluid decreases.

The discovery of the relationship between motion and pressure became known as Bernoulli's principle. Place a strip of paper below your lips and blow. The strip of paper rises because the pressure of the still air under it is greater than the pressure of the moving air coming from your lungs. Increasing the speed causes the pressure to drop. Like the strip of paper, roofs are lifted off buildings during windstorms because of the lower pressure above the roof.

As Daniel worked in Basel, he learned disturbing news. It concerned his father, Johann. During his years in Russia, his father had intentionally blocked his return to Switzerland. Johann had enjoyed the reputation as one of the greatest mathematicians in the world. He was certainly the greatest mathematician in Basel. He did not want his famous son to come back and take that title away from him.

In 1734, Johann received word that he had received the prize given by the Paris Academy of Science for the most important scientific advance of the previous year. Unfortunately, the award went jointly to himself and his son Daniel.

Rather than rejoicing at Daniel's success, Johann resented his son's achievements. When Daniel visited his father, a loud argument broke out. His father accused Daniel of stealing his mathematical ideas. Johann threw Daniel out of the house and told him never to come back.

Daniel tried to patch up the argument. In 1737 he wrote a book about his studies of fluids in motion. He published it as *Hydrodynamica* by Daniel Bernoulli, Son of Johann. His efforts to honor his father and soften Johann's heart failed.

Sadly, Johann died in 1748 never having spoken to his son again. A heartsick Daniel gave up mathematics in favor of medicine and other areas of science.

8

THE BLIND MASTER

S uppose scientists were judged by their scientific output. The Swiss mathematician Leonhard Euler (pronounced Oiler) would be at the top of the list. He wrote more than 800 research papers and 31 books. Some were large and thick books. Despite the number, his discoveries were first-rate. Even more remarkable, about half of his work was done while he was totally blind.

Euler was born in Basel, Switzerland, in 1707. His father, Paul Euler, served as a minister in the nearby village of Riechen. Paul Euler had received a good education at Basel and had taken mathematics under Jacob Bernoulli, Daniel Bernoulli's uncle. Paul enrolled his son at the University of Basel in Switzerland.

Leonhard Euler planned to become a minister of the gospel like his father. At the university, he studied theology and Hebrew. He earned an advanced college degree at the early age of 17.

Euler came under the influence of the Bernoulli family. Although he studied for the ministry, he began taking courses in mathematics. The Bernoullis pitched in and gave him private instruction in the subject.

His father insisted that Leonhard put aside his mathematical studies to prepare for the ministry.

The Bernoullis' spoke privately with the father. They said, "Your son Leonhard will become a great mathematician."

Leonhard Euler (1707–1783) first studied for the clergy at the Swiss University in Basel. There the famed Johann Bernoulli noticed his skill in mathematics and encouraged him to change his career. Euler became one of the great mathematicians of all time.

Reluctantly, Paul Euler agreed to let his son major in mathematics.

Leonhard Euler studied mathematics at Basel until he became Daniel Bernoulli's assistant in St. Petersburg. Catherine I paid Euler a salary by making him a medical officer in the Russian navy. Switzerland had no navy, and the only sailing ship Euler had ever seen were boats on the Swiss lakes. Nevertheless, he found himself a member of the Russian navy with a rank of lieutenant.

He and Daniel became fast friends. He lived with Daniel Bernoulli until 1733. Then he married and left the Bernoulli home. Daniel went back to Basel. Euler filled in behind Daniel and became professor of mathematics at the Academy of Science.

Unfortunately, Catherine I died shortly after Euler arrived, and life in Russia became grim because of political turmoil. Those who spoke against the government were thrown into prison. The government became suspicious of foreigners. The secret police followed Euler everywhere.

Euler fell into the habit of continually being busy. In that way, he had an excuse to avoid appearances at the palace. A chance remark might land him and his family in jail. He took on any assignment that came his way. He oversaw reform of the country's weights and measures, designed water pumps for fire engines, and wrote mathematics textbooks for elementary school.

He supervised the making of Russian maps. Mapmaking was a mathematical and geometric art. The earth had a spherical surface with three dimensions. A map portrayed that surface on a sheet of flat paper with two dimensions. Surveyors took measurements in the field. Converting their measurements into useful maps took exceptional skill.

Euler's powers of concentration were legendary. He was a devoted father who loved to have his children around him even as he worked. He had a large family. At one time 18 family members lived in his household. Children would play in the same room with him while he developed the most complicated mathematical equations. Sometimes he would rock a baby to sleep as he wrote one of his many books.

He said, "I make some of my best discoveries while holding a baby in my arm with other children playing around my feet."

His early training as a minister served him well with his large family. He conducted the family devotion each night. He would give a short talk about some Bible subject. He led prayers and gave thanks for God's blessings.

In 1738 he spent nearly three days in intense concentration on a problem in astronomy. He became ill, one of his eyes became infected, and he lost his sight in that eye. That setback hardly affected his work as a mathematician.

In 1740, Russia was plunged again into uncertainty because of the death of the current ruler. At that decisive moment, Fredrick the Great of Prussia invited Euler to Berlin. Euler quickly accepted.

In Berlin, Euler was expected to spend time at the palace. Euler did not enjoy court life and usually stood silently away from the whirl of activity. Frederick the Great's mother complained that he was strangely silent. Euler said, "I have just come from a country where people who speak out of turn are hanged."

The Berlin Academy of Sciences paid so well that he was able to afford a home in Berlin and a farm in the country.

Russia continued to pay him a salary, too. The fact that Russia and Prussia both claimed Leonhard Euler was even more remarkable because the two countries constantly fought one another. In one battle, the Russian army burned Euler's country estate. Russia apologized and paid him for his loss. Not to be outdone, Fredrick the Great also paid Euler a similar sum.

Euler continued to conduct the nightly devotion for his family and say a prayer of thanksgiving. Euler believed he had much for which to be thankful. Few people could earn livings as mathematicians. Yet, Euler received a salary from not one country but two. They paid him quite well.

During this time he realized the leaders of Fredrick the Great's country had a poor education in science. Euler decided to remedy the situation by writing a book on the rudiments of science and mathematics. However, he knew that adults were reluctant to admit their ignorance. They would resent it if he wrote as if teaching common school children. How could he teach about science without talking down to his readers?

Euler found a solution by pretending to write his book for one of Frederick's nieces. He called it *Letters to a German Princess*. She was known not to have any scientific training. Euler could explain in detail the basics of science and mathematics without offending his adult audience. His book became immensely popular. It circulated throughout Prussia and was translated into seven languages.

Mathematics can be pure or applied. Applied mathematics answers questions of immediate interest such as how to convert weights and measures, make maps, build bridges, and design ships. Pure mathematics investigates numbers without any particular real-life application. Rulers such as Fredrick the Great expected Euler to study practical problems, but they understood that pure research was important, too. Euler would often take up mathematical puzzles simply because he enjoyed the challenges.

For instance, the citizens of Königsberg, on the banks of the Pregel River had an interesting puzzle. The city occupied both banks of the river as well as two islands in the river. In all, seven bridges connected the various parts of the city. The people who took a Sunday stroll wondered if they could find a path through the city that would cross all seven bridges only once. No one succeeded.

This was the kind of puzzle that Euler enjoyed.

He reduced the city, islands, and bridges to a simple diagram. He noted that the smaller island had three bridges connected to it. With just three bridges, if a person started on the island, then he would leave it by one bridge, return by a second bridge and then leave again by the third bridge. If a person started elsewhere then he had to enter the island by one bridge, leave by another bridge, and return by the third bridge. He would end up on the island.

"A person cannot both begin and end on the small island," Euler realized. "If a person begins on the small island, then he finishes elsewhere. If he begins elsewhere, then he must finish on the island."

He looked at the north shore. It also had three bridges. A person had to either begin there or end there but could not do both. The south shore also had three bridges. The person had to begin there or end there, too. *But wait*, Euler thought, *a path has only one ending point. No matter where a person starts, he must end at two different places and that is impossible.*

To walk across all seven bridges without crossing one a second time was impossible.

When he solved the Königsberg bridge problem, Euler developed the tools to solve similar problems. He started a whole new field of mathematics known as network

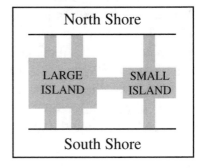

North Shore

LARGE ISLAND

SMALL ISLAND

South Shore

design. The importance of this field became even more important with the invention of the telephone, computers, and the Internet.

One of Euler's special skills was to develop an algorithm for solving problems. An algorithm is the procedure that leads to a solution. Often, a mathematician could arrive at an answer to a particular problem, but the same procedure would not solve a similar problem. At other times he found a solution, but only the most intelligent and skilled mathematician could repeat the steps.

Euler developed an algorithm for solving related problems. His algorithms were so easy to follow that even a beginning math student could solve new problems of the same type. As the industrial revolution changed how people worked, this step-by-step, problem-solving method became very important. Ordinary citizens found themselves in jobs that required the ability to solve problems. Euler's algorithms allowed people with ordinary abilities to arrive at answers to complicated problems.

Today, microprocessors do calculations. Despite the advances, the computer program in the central processing unit is run by software based on mathematical algorithms.

As the years passed, Fredrick the Great became more difficult to serve. Euler was a simple man who did not enjoy the rich dress and idle conversation of court life. Some people enjoyed verbal duels. They pretended to be friendly, but edged the conversation with cutting remarks. Euler was repelled by the sneaky and dishonest activity in Fredrick the Great's court.

Meanwhile, Catherine the Great became the new ruler of Russia. She began as a generous and farsighted ruler. At the start of her reign, she allowed local self-government. Even the peasants had a role in managing their affairs. She invited Euler back to Russia and he accepted.

She welcomed Euler by setting aside a house big enough for his large family. She delegated one of her cooks to his service. Euler became the director of the Academy of Sciences in St. Petersburg.

One of the reasons that Catherine the Great invited Euler to her court was to counter the arguments of Denis Diderot who did not believe in God. Catherine the Great had invited Diderot to Russia because he had almost single-handedly written a large encyclopedia. She made Diderot the director of her library. However, Diderot soon proved worrisome. He was a determined atheist who tried to convert others to his unbelief.

Catherine the Great knew that Euler was a devout Christian. She believed a person of his stature would restore Christian balance to her court. Because Euler defended Christianity against the unbeliever, others took a stand, too. Fewer and fewer people were willing to listen to Diderot's rants against Christianity. After only five months, Diderot decided to resign his position and move back to France.

Euler's deep religious faith helped him as he became blind. Euler lost vision in one eye years earlier. Now he began going blind in the other eye. As the darkness closed in, he did not give up. He refused to let the tragedy slow him. He trained one of his sons, Albert, to take dictation and see the manuscript through the printers.

Incredibly, his production increased. He accomplished more in the 17 years he was totally blind than he did in the same period when he could see. His greatest triumph, the three-body problem, came after he lost his sight.

His remarkable memory was a great help in those trying days. After dictating six blackboards full of equations, he could go back through and repeat the dictation exactly.

One of his admirers said, "Euler calculated without apparent effort, as men breathe, or as eagles sustain themselves in the wind."

In Euler's day, knowing the exact orbit of the moon was important to sailing vessels. Captains of ships used the moon's location to plot their positions on the ocean. Calculating the moon's orbit involved three bodies: sun, moon, and earth.

Astronomers could easily calculate the gravitational attraction between the earth and moon or between the sun and moon. Gravitational force acting among three objects at once was very complex. No one had been able to calculate fully the gravitational tug of earth, moon, and sun upon one another. This was known as the three-body problem. The solution had escaped many great scientists, including Isaac Newton himself. "It is the only problem that made my head hurt," Newton said.

Euler's solution remained the best available for two hundred years. Euler's work in this area was especially important to the seafaring nation of Britain. That country depended upon accurate navigation because of its far-flung empire. Britain was so impressed with Euler's solution that they sent him an award of 300 pounds for his efforts. At that time, a working family could live for a year on a salary of 50 pounds.

Leonhard Euler worked up to the very moment he died. On the afternoon of September 18, 1783, he investigated the science of hot air balloons. These lighter-than-air craft were recent inventions. They'd been shown in public only six months earlier. How they worked was not well understood.

After dinner, Euler turned to the orbit of Uranus. William Herschel had announced the discovery of this planet a year earlier. Astronomers needed widely spaced observations to calculate an orbit. Such observations did not exist for Uranus because it moved so slowly. Euler calculated the orbit using limited observations.

One of his grandsons entered. Euler put aside his work. He played with the boy. Along about evening teatime, everything seemed normal. Leonhard Euler sat back, relaxed, and drank his tea. In the space of one breath to the next, Euler suffered a stroke and died.

When he died, the printer still had volumes of material on hand. He could publish a new paper each month for the next 30 years. Leonhard Euler wrote more research papers than any other mathematician, perhaps more than any other scientist. When a list is made of the greatest mathematicians of all time, Leonhard Euler is usually near the top of the list.

9

PRINCE OF
MATHEMATICIANS

C arl Friedrich Gauss was born of poor parents in a cottage in Brunswich, Germany. His father worked hard as a gardener. The young Gauss had a great memory. By the time he was three, he had learned his letters and numbers.

One Saturday morning, his father figured the pay for the gardeners. The three-year-old boy watched carefully. When his father finished, little Carl Gauss cried, "Father, the reckoning is wrong." The boy then gave the correct answer.

Carl Gauss began school at age seven. Two years passed before he took a class in arithmetic. The instructor gave a long addition problem to the class. It should have kept them busy for an hour. Carl instantly wrote the answer on his slate. He alone had the correct answer.

The young scholar had seen a short cut. Suppose you are asked to add the numbers 1, 2, 3, 4, and so on to 100. There is a quick way. Notice that $1 + 100 = 101$; $2 + 99 = 101$; $3 + 98 = 101$; and so on to $50 + 51 = 101$. This gives 50 pairs of numbers, each with a sum of 101. The final total of the sum for the first 100 numbers is 50 times 101, or 5,050.

The instructor had given a much more difficult problem. But it could be quickly worked in the same way. His teacher said, "He is beyond me. I can teach him nothing more." The

Carl Gauss

teacher bought a book on mathematics and gave it to his star ten-year-old pupil. He arranged for an assistant to work through the book with the boy.

Carl's father expected his son to take up a trade such as bricklayer or gardener. Carl's uncle recognized the boy's genius. Uncle Friedrich knew that a tradesman could lead a happy and fulfilling life. For his nephew, however, he wanted more. He and Carl's teacher asked the Duke of Brunswick for help. The Duke asked to talk with Carl. The boy's humility and evident intelligence won the Duke's heart. The Duke agreed to pay for the boy's education.

Carl Gauss lived in the days before computers or pocket calculators. He did all calculations in his head or with pen and paper. Logarithms were one short cut. Logarithms changed multiplication and division into easier addition and subtraction. To make his calculations go faster, Gauss memorized a table of logarithms. The table had ten thousand numbers each of four digits.

Prime numbers fascinated Gauss. The prime numbers are 2, 3, 5, 7, 11, 13, and so. A prime number is divisible only by itself and one. Two is the only even prime number. One is not considered a prime number.

A composite number is the name given to whole numbers that are not prime. A composite number can be made as the product of prime numbers. Fifteen is a composite number. It can be written as $15 = 3 * 5$ and both 3 and 5 are prime.

Mathematicians believed that multiplying prime numbers together could make every composite number and that it could only be done in one way. For instance, 36 is 2 * 2 * 3 * 3. No other group of prime numbers multiplied together will give 36. It is easy to see this for a small number such as 36. The idea that multiplying prime numbers together can make composite numbers is called the fundamental theorem of arithmetic. Mathematicians all the way back to Euclid believed this to be true. However, none of them could prove it. Gauss was the first mathematician to prove the fundamental theorem of arithmetic.

His most public triumph came because of a lost planet.

John Bode, a German astronomer, convinced other astronomers that a planet had to orbit between Mars and Jupiter. Bode had found a sequence of numbers that seemed to show there was a gap between Mars and Jupiter that should have a planet. He came to this conclusion while studying the positions of the known planets. He used earth's distance as a measuring guide and set it equal to 10. The planets were at distances of 4 (Mercury), 7 (Venus), 10 (Earth), 17 (Mars), 52 (Jupiter), and 100 (Saturn). The numbers 4, 7, 10, 17, 52, and 100 had a big gap between 17 and 52. Was there a planet at that distance that had gone unnoticed?

Bode believed the missing planet would be at a distance of 28 from the sun. He got that number in this way. First, he took the numbers 0, 3, 6, 12, 24, 48, and 96, doubling each one. Next, he added four: 4, 7, 10, 16, 28, 52, and 100. All of the planets matched the numbers in the sequence except for 28. John Bode predicted a planet would be at that distance from the sun.

Astronomers made plans for a thorough search of the sky for John Bode's planet.

An astronomer who was not a member of the search team beat them to the discovery. His name was Giuseppe Piazzi.

On January 1, 1801, while working on another matter, Piazzi came across a dim planet. Piazzi fell sick before he could make enough observations to calculate its orbit. When he got well, he eagerly returned to the telescope. The little planet had moved into the daytime sky and couldn't be seen.

Had he lost it forever? Piazzi's observations were few in number and very inexact. Astronomers concluded that calculating an orbit was impossible.

Carl Gauss decided to try his hand at it. He tackled this problem with a mathematical trick of his own invention, called the method of least squares. Using this tool, he calculated the orbit of the lost planet. The new planet returned to the night sky. Astronomers found it at the position Carl Gauss predicted.

They named the new planet Ceres. It was tiny. Most planets are thousands of miles in diameter. Ceres is less than 500 miles across. Even in a powerful telescope, it was a pinpoint of light like a star. They called it an asteroid, which means starlike. Other astronomers preferred the name "minor planet." Later, they found other asteroids or minor planets between Mars and Jupiter.

Carl Gauss' method of least squares has proven to be a resounding success. It is in daily use by scientists all around the world. It has become one of the most important mathematical tools ever invented. It has become far more important than the little planet it helped find.

In 1806, Gauss became the director of an observatory in Germany. Measuring positions in the heavens required that the observatory's position be very accurately known. Gauss learned about surveying. He developed better ways to measure positions on earth.

He studied the size and shape of the earth. He grew interested in the earth's magnetic field. He calculated the location of the earth's magnetic poles. Earth's magnetic poles are located several hundred miles from true north.

Gauss and a friend built an electromagnetic relay for sending messages from his home to the observatory. He'd made a working telegraph, but made no effort to publicize the invention.

He often made discoveries that he kept to himself. For instance, he recorded his most important discoveries in a notebook. During 16 years he entered 146 brief notes about his discoveries. The notebook contained enough discoveries to make the reputations of a half-dozen people.

He also developed a new type of geometry, the first one since the time of Euclid. It began as Gauss questioned the parallel postulate. As you know, Euclid assumed that from a point not on a given line, one and only one line could be drawn parallel to the given line. It was from this assumption that Euclid developed the proof that the angles of a triangle sum to 180°. If a triangle has a 90-degree angle and a 50-degree angle, then the third angle must be 40 degrees: $90° + 50° + 40° = 180°$.

The parallel postulate does appear to agree with the real world. Gauss tested this observation. He used powerful telescopes and precise surveying equipment to measure the angles of triangles several miles on a side. The angles in each one totaled to 180°, which agreed with Euclid's geometry.

However, Gauss realized that the parallel postulate was only an assumption and that other assumptions were possible. For instance, he encouraged a young German mathematician, Bernhard Riemann, to investigate what would happen if through a given point not on a given line no line parallel to the given line could be drawn. In Riemann's geometry, space is curved. The shortest distance between two points is not a straight line. Instead, the shortest distance is a curve that fits the curved surface.

The idea of non-Euclidian geometry that Riemann advanced became a useful way of describing a gravity field when Einstein developed his theory of relativity. Riemann went on to develop several new concepts in mathematics and modern physics.

Bernhard Riemann was the son of a preacher of the gospel. Riemann wanted to be a minister, too. However, he had a ready grasp of mathematics and science. As a schoolboy, he designed a calendar that could give the day and date for any year — a perpetual calendar.

His college work began in Bible studies and Hebrew.

However, his God-given talents were obviously in mathematics. In addition, he was excessively shy. Speaking to an audience left him tongue-tied — not a trait that is helpful for a person who plans to fill a pulpit.

Although he made mathematical research his profession, Riemann continued to study the Bible throughout his life. He served God faithfully, as his father had, but in his own way. Because of the poverty of his childhood, Riemann had been poorly nourished. He often became sick. He died at age 39. His wife was at his side holding his hand. He felt the end coming and began reciting the Lord's Prayer. He died while saying the words "Forgive us our trespasses." His tombstone has the line, "All things work together for good to them that love God" (Rom. 8:28).

Carl Gauss' encouragement to Bernhard Riemann was one of his many successes. Unlike some scientists who become set in their ways as they grow older, Gauss always welcomed new ideas from his students. Throughout his life, he learned languages to exercise his mind. At age 60, he took up Russian. He learned to read, write, and speak it flawlessly. Those who didn't know better assumed he'd had a tutor to help him. He'd learned the language without any assistance.

One advantage of learning new languages was that he could read the best books in each country's native tongue. His friends could tell when he had read books with unhappy endings. His sensitive nature would cause him to be upset for days afterward.

Gauss became known as the Prince of Mathematicians. Despite his fame, he lived a simple life. He worked in a small, unheated study with a little worktable and shaded lamp. He ate plain food and dressed in a warm robe and a velvet cap.

Carl Gauss was happy that his mother enjoyed his many successes. When she became elderly, he welcomed her into his home. She lived with him for 22 years. At age 93 she became blind. Carl Gauss allowed no one but himself to care for her. She died at age 97.

Carl Friedrich Gauss died in 1855 at the age of 77. During

his lifetime he was asked to name the great mathematicians. He named Archimedes and Isaac Newton. Now a third name is added to the list — that of his own.

A

Achilles 8
algorithm 60
Archimedes 23–27, 43
Aristotle 43
asteroid 66
astronomy 8
Ayscough, William 35

B

Barlow, Professor 36
Bate, John 34
Bernoulli, Daniel 47–53
Bernoulli, Jacob 44–46
Bernoulli, Johann 44, 47, 53
Bernoulli, Nicolaus 44
Bernoulli's principle 52
binomial 36
Black Death 36
blood pressure 51
Bode, John 65
Bonacci, Guilielmo 28
Book of Calculating 29
Boyle, Robert 44

C

Caesar, Julius 15
calculus 38–39
catenary 45
Catherine I 50
Catherine the Great 60–61
Ceres 66
chambered nautilus 30
circle 37
composite number 64–65
computers 18
Copernicus 21
Cromwell, Oliver 33
cycloid 44

D

da Vinca, Leonardo 43
David 10
diagonal 12
Diderot, Denis 61
Duke of Brunswick 64

E

eclipse 8
Einstein, Albert 15, 22

electromagnetic relay 66
elements 19
Elements of Geometry 15
Elephantine Island 21
ellipse 37
encrypted 18
energy 51–52
Eratosthenes 43
Euclid 9, 15–22, 43
Euler, Leonhard 50–51, 55–62

F

Fibonacci, Leonardo 28–31
Fibonacci series 30–31
Fredrick the Great 57
fundamental theorem of arithmetic 65

G

Galileo 21, 39–40, 43
Gauss, Carl Friedrich 63–69
Gelon 26
gravity 40–42

H

Halley, Edmund 41, 44
Harvey, William 49
Herschel, William 62
Hieron II 23
Hiram 7
Homer 8
Hooke, Robert 44
hourglass 49
Hydrodynamica 53
hyperbola 37
hypotenuse 11

I

Imperial Academy 50
Internet 18, 60
irrational number 13

J

Jacob 44–46

K

Kepler, Johannes 39–40
King Charles I 33
King Saul 10
Königsberg bridge 59

L

law of conservation of energy 52

laws of motion 48–49
Leaning Tower of Pisa 28
Letters to a German Princess 58
logarithms 64
Lord Protector 34
Lydians 8

M
magnetic poles 66
Malpighi, Marcello 43
mapmaking 57
Marcellius, Marcus Claudis 26
Matthew's law 43
Medes 8
method of least squares 66
myriad 26
Mysteries of Nature and Art 34

N
network design 59
Newton, Isaac 15, 21, 33–42, 44
non-Euclidian geometry 67

O
Odesseus 8
On the Motion of the Heart and Blood 49
optics 19

P
parabola 37
parallel postulate 21
Paris Academy of Science 47
Peter the Great 50
pi 13, 24
Piazzi, Giuseppe 65–66
place value 29
Plato 17, 43
Plutarch 26
polygon 24–25
postulate 21
prime numbers 18, 64–65
Prince of Mathematicians 68
Principia Mathematica 41–42
printing press 21
Ptolemy 17
pyramids 8
Pythagoras 7–14
Pythagorean theorem 11

Q
Queen Anne 42

R
rational numbers 12
Riemann, Bernhard 67–68
right triangle 11
Royal Society 44

S
Sand Reckoner, The 26
Second Punic War 26
Smith, Barnabas 33
Socrates 43
software 60
Some Mathematical Exercises 50

T
telegraph 66
Thales 8
three-body problem 61
Trojan wars 8

U
University of Padua 44, 49
Uranus 62

W
Washington, George 15
Westminster Abbey 42
Wren, Christopher 44

Z
zero 29